SEVEN WORDS

of

JESUS AND MARY

By

RT. REV. FULTON J. SHEEN
Ph.D., D.D., LL.D., Litt.D.

*Agrégé en philosophie de l'Université de
Louvain, and The Catholic
University of America*

Martino Fine Books
Eastford, CT

2017

Martino Fine Books
P.O. Box 913,
Eastford, CT 06242 USA

ISBN 978-1-68422-088-5

Copyright 2017
Martino Fine Books

Cover Design Tiziana Matarazzo

Printed in the United States of America On 100% Acid-Free Paper

SEVEN WORDS
of
JESUS AND MARY

By

RT. REV. FULTON J. SHEEN
Ph.D., D.D., LL.D., Litt.D.

*Agrégé en philosophie de l'Université de
Louvain, and The Catholic
University of America*

NEW YORK
P. J. KENEDY & SONS

Nihil Obstat:

ARTHUR J. SCANLAN, S.T.D.
Censor Librorum

Imprimatur:

✠ FRANCIS J. SPELLMAN, **D.D.**
Archbishop of New York

New York, 1945
Feast of the Sacred Heart

DEDICATED

TO

MARY QUEEN OF THE HOLY ROSARY

GRACIOUS PATRONESS OF THE UNITED STATES

IN HUMBLE PETITION

THAT

THROUGH THY IMMACULATE HEART

THE WORLD MAY FIND ITS WAY BACK TO

THE SACRED HEART OF THY DIVINE SON

CONTENTS

THE FIRST WORD

The Value of Ignorance

CHAPTER I

THE FIRST WORD

The Value of Ignorance

ONE thousand years before Our Blessed Lord was born, there lived one of the greatest of all poets: the glorious Homer of the Greeks. Two great epics are ascribed to him: one the Iliad; the other, the Odyssey. The hero of the Iliad was not Achilles, but Hector, the leader of the enemy Trojans whom Achilles defeated and killed. The poem ends not with the glorification of Achilles but of the defeated Hector.

The other poem, the Odyssey, has as its hero, not Odysseus, but Penelope, his wife, who was faithful to him during the years of his travels. As the suitors pressed for her affections, she told them that when she finished weaving the garment they saw before her, she would listen to their courtship. But each night she unraveled what she had woven in the day, and thus remained faithful until her husband returned. "Of all women," she said, "I am the most sorrowful." Well might be applied to her the words of Shakespeare: "Sorrow sits in my soul as on a throne. Bid kings come and bow down to it."

For a thousand years before the birth of Our Blessed Lord, pagan antiquity resounded with these two stories of the poet who threw into the teeth of history the mysterious challenge of glorifying a defeated man and hailing a sorrowful woman. How, the subsequent centuries asked, could anyone be victorious in defeat and glorious in sorrow? And the answer was never given until that day when there came One Who was glorious in defeat: the Christ on His Cross; and one who was magnificent in sorrow: His Blessed Mother beneath the Cross.

It is interesting that Our Lord spoke seven times on Calvary and that His

Mother is recorded as having spoken but seven times in Sacred Scripture. Her last recorded word was at the Marriage Feast of Cana, when her Divine Son began His Public life. Now that the sun was out, there was no longer need of the moon to shine. Now that the Word has spoken, there was no longer need of words.

St. Luke records five of the seven words which he could have known only from her. St. John records the other two. One wonders, as Our Blessed Lord spoke each of His Seven Words, if Our Blessed Mother at the foot of the Cross did not think of each of her corresponding words. Such will be the subject of our meditation: Our Lord's Seven Words on the Cross and the Seven Words of Mary's life.

Men cannot stand weakness. Men are, in a certain sense, the weaker sex. There is nothing that so much unnerves a man as a woman's tears. Therefore men need the strength and the inspiration of women who do not break down in a crisis. They need someone not prostrate at the foot of the Cross, but standing, as Mary stood. John was there; he saw her standing, and he wrote it down in his Gospel.

Generally when innocent men suffer at the hands of impious judges, their last words are either: "I am innocent" or "The courts are rotten." But here for the first time in the hearing of the world, is one who asked neither for the forgiveness of His own sins, for He is God, nor proclaimed His own innocence, for men are not judges of God. Rather does He plead for those who kill Him: "Father, forgive them, for they know not what they do." (Luke 23:34).

Mary beneath the gibbet heard Her Divine Son speak that First Word. I wonder, when she heard Him say "know not" if she did not recall her own First Word. It, too, contained those words: "know not."

The occasion was the Annunciation, the first good news to reach the earth in centuries. The angel announced to her that she was to become the Mother of God:

"Behold thou shalt conceive in thy womb and shalt bring forth a son: and thou shalt call his name Jesus. He shall be great and shall be called the son of the Most High. And the Lord God shall give unto him the throne of David his father: and he shall reign in the house of Jacob for ever. And of his Kingdom there shall be no end. And Mary said to the Angel: How shall this be done, because I know not man?" (Luke 1:31-34)

These words of Jesus and Mary seem to suggest that there is sometimes wisdom in not knowing. Ignorance is here represented not as a cure, but a blessing. This rather shocks our modern sensibilities which so much glorify education, but that is because we fail to distinguish between true wisdom and false wisdom. St. Paul called the wisdom of the world "foolishness," and Our Blessed Lord thanked His Heavenly Father that He had not revealed Heavenly Wisdom to the worldly wise.

The ignorance which is here extolled is

not ignorance of the truth, but ignorance of evil. Notice it first of all in the word of Our Saviour to His executioners: He implied that they could be forgiven only because they were ignorant of their terrible crime. It was not their wisdom that would save them, but their ignorance.

If they knew what they were doing as they smote the Hands of Everlasting Mercy, dug the Feet of the Good Shepherd, crowned the Head of Wisdom Incarnate, and still went on doing it, they would never have been saved. They would have been damned! It was only their ignorance which brought them within the pale of redemption and forgiveness. As St. Peter told them on Pentecost: "I know that you did it through ignorance: as did also your rulers." (Acts 3:17)

Why is it that you and I, for example, can sin a thousand times and be forgiven, and the angels who have sinned but once, are eternally unforgiven? The reason is that the angels *knew* what they were doing. The angels see the consequences of

each and every one of their decisions with
the same clarity that you see that a part
can never be greater than the whole. Once
you make that judgment you can never
take it back. It is irrevocable; it is eternal.

Now the angels saw the consequences
of their choices with still greater clarity.
Therefore, when they made a decision,
they made it knowingly and there was no
taking it back. They were lost forever.
Tremendous are the responsibilities of
knowing! Those who know the truth will
be judged more severely than those who
know it not. As Our Blessed Lord said:
"If I had not come . . . they would not
have sin." (John 15:22)

The First Word Our Blessed Mother
spoke at the Annunciation revealed the
same lesson. She said: "I know not man."
Why was there a value in not knowing
man? Because she had consecrated her
virginity to God. At a moment when
every woman sought the privilege of being the Mother of the Messias, Mary gave
up the hope and received it. She refuses

to discuss with an angel any kind of compromise with her high resolve.

If the condition of becoming the Mother of God was the surrender of her vow, she would not make that surrender, knowing man would have been evil for her, though it would not have been evil in other circumstances. Not knowing man is a kind of ignorance, but here it proves to be such a blessing that in an instant the Holy Spirit overshadows her, making her a living ciborium privileged to bear within herself for nine months the Guest Who is the Host of the world.

These first words of Jesus and Mary suggest there is value in not knowing evil. You live in a world in which the wordly wise say: "You do not know life; you have never lived." They assume that you can know nothing except by experience—experience not only of good but of evil.

It was with this kind of lie that Satan tempted our First Parents. He told them that the reason God forbade them to eat of the tree of the knowledge of good and evil was because God did not want them to be wise as He was wise. Satan did not tell them that if they came to a knowledge of good and evil, it would be very different from God's knowledge.

God knows evil only abstractly, i.e., by negation of His Goodness and Love. But man would know it concretely and experimentally, and thus would to some extent fall captive to the very evil which he experienced. God wanted our first parents to know typhoid fever, for example, as a healthy doctor knows it; He did not want them to know it as the stricken patient knows it. And from that day of the Great Lie, down to this, no one is better because he knows evil through experience.

Examine your own life. If you know evil by experience, are you wiser because of it? Have you not despised that very evil and are you not the more tragic for having experienced it? You may even have become mastered by the evil you experienced. How often the disillusioned say: "I wish I had never tasted liquor," or "I regret the day I stole my first dollar," and "I wish I had never known that person." How much wiser you would have been had you been ignorant!

Over and over again when you broke some law which you thought arbitrary and meaningless, you discovered the principle which dictated it. As a child you could not understand why your parents forbade you to play with matches, but the burn convinced you of the truth of the law. So the world by violating God's moral law is finding through war, strife, and misery, the wisdom of the law. How it would now like to unlearn its false learning!

Think not, then, that in order to "know life" you must "experience evil." Is a doctor wiser because he is prostrate with disease? Do we know cleanliness by living in sewers? Do we know education by experiencing stupidity? Do we know peace by fighting? Do we know the joys of vision by being blinded? Do you become a better pianist by hitting the wrong keys?

You do not need to get drunk to know what drunkenness is.

Do not excuse yourself by saying "temptations are too strong," or "good people do not know what temptation is." The good know more about the strength of temptations than those who fall. How do you know how strong the current of a river is? By swimming with the current or by swimming against it? How do you know how strong the enemy is in battle? By being captured or by conquering? How can you know the strength of a temptation unless you overcome it? Our Blessed Lord really understands the power of temptation better than anyone, because He overcame the temptations of Satan.

The great fallacy of modern education is the assumption that the reason there is evil in the world is because there is ignorance, and that if we pour more facts in the minds of the young we will make them better. If this were true, we should be the most virtuous people in the history of the world, because we are the best educated.

The facts, however, point the other way: Never before has there been so much education and never before so little coming to the knowledge of the truth. We forget that ignorance is better than error. *Scientia* is not *sapientia*. Much of modern education is making the mind sceptical about the Wisdom of God. The young are not born sceptics, but a false education can make them sceptical. The modern world is dying of sceptic poisoning.

The fallacy of sex education is assuming that if children know the evil effects of certain acts, they will abstain from those acts. It is argued that if you knew there was typhoid fever in a house you would not go into that house. But what these educators forget is that the sex-appeal is not at all like the typhoid fever appeal. No person has an urge to break down the doors of a typhoid patient, but the same cannot be said about sex. There is a sex-impulse but there is no typhoid instinct.

Sex wisdom does not necessarily make one wise; it can make one desire the evil,

particularly when we learn that the evil
effects can be avoided. Sex Hygiene is not
morality. Soap is not the same as virtue.
Badness comes not from our ignorance of
knowing, but from our perversity of doing.

That is why in our Catholic schools we
train and discipline the will as well as in-
form the intellect, because we know that
character is in our choices, not in our
knowing. All of us already *know* enough
to be good, even before we start to school.
What we have to learn is how to *do
better*.

If we forget the burden of our fallen
nature, and the accumulated proneness
to evil that comes from submitting to it,
we soon become chained as Samson was
and all the education in the world cannot
break those chains. Education may conceivably rationalize the chains and make
us believe they are charms, but only the
effort of the will plus the grace of God
can free us from their servitude. Without
those two energies we will never do one

jot or tittle beyond that which we have already done.

Train your children and yourself, then, in the true wisdom which is the knowledge of God, and in the ignorance of the things that are evil. The unknown is the undesired; to be ignorant of wickedness is not to desire it. There are no joys like Innocence.

Here on the Cross and on its shadow were the two most Innocent Persons of all history: Jesus was absolutely sinless because He is the Son of God; Mary was Immaculate because she was preserved free from original sin, in virtue of the merits of her Divine Son. It was their innocence which made their sufferings so keen.

People living in dirt hardly ever realize how dirty dirt is. Those who live in sin hardly understand the horror of sin. The one peculiar and terrifying thing about sin is, the more experience you have with it, the less you know about it. You become so identified with it, that you know neither the depths to which you have sunk nor the heights from which you have fallen.

You never know you were asleep until you wake up; and you never know the horror of sin until you get out of sin. Hence, only the sinless really know what sin is. And since here on the Cross and beneath it, there is Innocence at its highest, it follows that there was also the greatest sorrow. Since there was no sin, there was the greatest understanding of its evil. It was their innocence, or their ignorance of evil, which made the agonies of Calvary.

To Jesus Who forgave those who "know not," to Mary who won God because she could say "I know not," pray that you may know not evil and thus be good.

Honestly, if you had the choice now either of learning more about the world, or of unlearning the evil you know, would you not rather unlearn than learn? Would you not be better if you were stripped of your wickedness than if you were clothed in the sheepskin of diplomas?

Would you not like to be right now just as you came from the hands of God at the baptismal font, with no worldly wisdom yet gathered to your mind, so that like an empty chalice, you might spend your life filling it with the wine of His Love? The world would call you ignorant, saying you knew nothing about life. Do not believe it —you would have Life! Therefore you would be one of the wisest persons in the world.

There is so much error in the world to-day, there are such vast areas of experienced and lived evil, that it would be a blessing if some generous soul would endow a University for Unlearning. Its purpose would be to do with error and evil exactly what doctors do with disease.

Would you be surprised to know that Our Lord did actually institute such a University for Unlearning, and to it all devout Catholics go about once a month? It is called the Confessional! You will not

be given a sheepskin when you walk out
of that confessional, but you will feel like
a lamb because Christ is your Shepherd.
You will be amazed at how much you will
learn by unlearning. It is easier for God
to write on a blank page than on one
covered with your scribblings.

THE SECOND WORD

The Secret of Sanctity

CHAPTER II

THE SECOND WORD

The Secret of Sanctity

THERE is only one thing in the world that is definitely and absolutely your own, and that is your will. Health, power, possessions and honor can all be snatched from you, but your will is irrevocably your own, even in hell. Hence, nothing really matters in life, except what you do with your will. It is that which makes the story of the two thieves crucified on either side of Our Lord, for here is the drama of wills.

Both thieves at first blasphemed. There was no such thing as the good thief at the beginning of the Crucifixion. But when the thief on the right heard that Man on the Central Cross forgive His executioners, he had a change of soul.

He began to accept his sorrows. He took

up his cross as a yoke rather than as a gibbet, abandoned himself to God's Will, and turning to the rebellious thief on the left said: "Neither dost thou fear God, seeing thou art under the same condemnation? And we indeed justly: for we receive the due reward of our deeds. But this man hath done no evil." (Luke 23:40-41)

Then from his heart already so full of surrender to His Saviour, there came this plea, "Remember me when thou shalt come into thy kingdom." (Luke 23:42) Immediately there came the answer: "Amen I say to thee: this day thou shalt be with me in paradise." (Luke 23:43)

"Thou." We are all individuals in the sight of God. He called His sheep by name. This word was the foundation of Christian democracy. Every soul is precious in God's sight, even those whom the State casts out and kills.

At the foot of the Cross, Mary witnessed the conversion of the good thief, and her soul rejoiced that he had accepted the Will of God. Her Divine Son's second word promising Paradise as a reward for that surrender, reminded her of her own Second Word thirty years before, when the angel had appeared to her and told her that she was to be the Mother of Him Who was now dying on the Cross.

In her First Word she asked how this would be accomplished since she knew not man. But when the angel said she would conceive of the Holy Spirit, Mary immediately answered: "Be it done to me according to thy word." *Fiat mihi* secundum verbum tuum. (Luke 1:38)

This was one of the great Fiats of the world. The first was at Creation when God said: *Fiat Lux:* "Let there be light;" another was in Gethsemani, when the Saviour pressing the chalice of redemption to His lips, cried: *Fiat voluntas tua:* "Thy will be done." (Matt. 26:42) The third was Mary's, pronounced in a Nazarene cottage, which proved to be a declaration of war against the empire of evil: *Fiat mihi* secundum verbum tuum. "Be it done to me according to thy word." (Luke 1:38)

The Second Word of Jesus on Golgotha and the second Word of Mary in Nazareth teach the same lesson: *Everyone in the world has a cross, but the cross is not the same for any two of us.* The cross of the thief was not the cross of Mary. The difference was due to God's will toward each. The thief was to give life; Mary to accept life. The thief was to hang on his cross; Mary was to stand beneath hers. The thief was to go ahead; Mary to remain behind. The thief received a dismissal; Mary received a mission. The thief was to be received into Paradise, but Paradise was to be received into Mary.

Each of us, too, has a cross. Our Lord said: "If any man will follow me." (Mark 8:34) He did not say: "Take up My Cross." My cross is not the same as yours, and yours is not the same as mine. Every cross in the world is tailor made, custom built, patterned to fit one and no one else.

That is why we say: "My cross is hard."

We assume that other persons' crosses are lighter, forgetful that the only reason our cross is hard is simply because it is our own. Our Lord did not make His Cross; it was made for Him. So yours is made by the circumstances of your life, and by your routine duties. That is why it fits so tightly. Crosses are not made by machines.

Our Lord deals separately with each soul. The crown of gold we want may have underneath it the crown of thorns, but the heroes who choose the crown of thorns often find that underneath it is the crown of gold. Even those that seem to be without a cross actually have one.

No one would have ever suspected that when Mary resigned herself to God's Will by accepting the honor of becoming the Mother of God, she would ever have to bear a cross. It would seem, too, that one who was preserved free from original sin should be dispensed from the penalties of that sin, such as pain. Yet this honor brought to her seven crosses and ended by making her the Queen of Martyrs.

There are, therefore, as many kinds of crosses as there are persons: crosses of grief and sorrow, crosses of want, crosses of abuse, crosses of wounded love and crosses of defeat.

There is the cross of widows. How often Our Lord spoke of them, for example, in the parable of the judge and the widow (Luke 18: 1-8); when He rebuked the Pharisees who "devour the houses of widows" (Mark 12:40); when He spoke to the widow of Naim (Luke 7:12), and when He praised the widow who threw two mites into the temple treasury. (Mark 12:42) Widowhood may have been particularly dear to Him, because His own mother was a widow, for Joseph His foster-father was presumably already dead.

When God takes someone from us, it is always for a good reason. When the sheep have grazed and thinned the grass in the lower regions, the shepherd will take a little lamb in his arms, carry it up the mountain where the grass is green, lay it down, and soon the other sheep will follow. Every now and then Our Lord takes a lamb from the parched field of a family up to those Heavenly Green pastures, that the rest of the family may keep their eyes on their true home and follow through.

Then there is the cross of sickness which always has a Divine purpose. Our Blessed Lord said: "This sickness is not unto death, but for the glory of God: that the Son of God may be glorified by it." (John 11:4) Resignation to this particular kind of cross is one of the very highest forms of prayer. Unfortunately, the sick generally want to be doing something else other than the thing that God wants them to do.

The tragedy of this world is not so much the pain in it; the tragedy is that so much of it is wasted. It is only when a log is thrown into the fire that it begins to sing. It was only when the thief was thrown into the fire of a cross that he began to find God. It is only in pain that some begin to discover where Love is.

Because our crosses differ, soul will differ from soul in glory. We think too often that in Heaven there is going to be somewhat the same equality in social positions that we have here; that servants on earth will be servants in heaven; that the important people on earth will be the important people in heaven. This is not true.

God will take into account our crosses. He seemed to suggest that in the parable of Dives and Lazarus: "Son, remember that thou didst receive good things in thy lifetime, and likewise Lazarus evil things: but now he is comforted and thou art tormented." (Luke 16:25)

There will be a bright jewel of merit for those who suffer in this world. Because we live in a world where position is determined economically, we forget that in God's world the royalty are those who do His Will; Heaven will be a complete reversal of values of earth. The first shall be last and the last first, for God is no respecter of persons.

A wealthy and socially important woman went to heaven. St. Peter pointed to a beautiful mansion and said: "This is your chauffeur's home." "Well," said she, "if that is his home, think what mine will be like." Pointing to a tiny cottage, Peter said: "There is yours." "I can't live in that," she answered. And Peter said: "I'm sorry, that is the best I could do with the material you sent me." Those who suffer as the thief did have sent ahead some fine material.

It makes no difference what you do here on earth; what matters is the love with which you do it. The street cleaner who accepts in God's name a cross arising from his state in life, such as the scorn of his fellowmen; the mother who pronounces her *Fiat* to the Divine Will as she raises a family for the Kingdom of God; the afflicted in hospitals who say *Fiat* to their cross of suffering are the uncanonized saints, for what is sanctity but fixation in goodness by abandonment to God's Holy Will?

It is typically American to feel that we are not doing anything unless we are doing something *big*. But from the Christian point of view, there is no one thing that is bigger than any other thing. The bigness comes from the way our wills utilize things. Hence mopping an office for the love of God is bigger than running the office for the love of money.

Most of our misery and unhappiness come from rebellion against our present state coupled with false ambition. We become critical of everyone above us, as if the cloak of honor which another wears was stolen from our shoulders. Rest assured that if it is God's Will that we do a certain task, it will be done, though the whole world would rise up and say "Nay." But if we get that honor by the abandonment of truth and humility, it will be bitter as wormwood and as biting as gall.

Each of us is to praise and love God in his own way. The bird praises God by singing, the flower by blooming, the clouds with their rain, the sun with its light, the moon with its reflection, and each of us by the patient resignation to the trials of his state in life.

In what does your life consist except two things? 1) Active duties. 2) Passive circumstances. The first is under your control; these do in God's name. The second is outside your control; these submit to in God's name. Consider only the present; leave the past to God's Justice, the future to His Providence. Perfection of personality does not consist in knowing God's plan, but in submitting to it as it reveals itself in the circumstances of life.

There is really one short cut to sanctity; the one Mary chose in the Visitation, the one Our Lord chose in Gethsemani, the one the thief chose on the Cross —abandonment to the Divine Will.

If the gold in the bowels of the earth did not say *Fiat* to the miner and the goldsmith, it would never become the chalice of the altar. If the pencil did not say *Fiat* to the hand of the writer, we would never have the poem; if Our Lady did not say *Fiat* to the angel, she would

never have become the House of Gold;
if Our Lord did not say *Fiat* to the
Father's Will in Gethsemani, we would
never have been redeemed; if the thief
did not say *Fiat* in his heart, he never
would have been the escort for the Master
into Paradise.

The reason most of us are what we are,
mediocre Christians, "up" one day,
"down" the next, is simply because we
refuse to let God work on us. As crude
marble we rebel against the hand of the
sculptor; as unvarnished canvas we shrink
from the oils and tints of the Heavenly
Artists. We are so "fearful lest having
Him we may have nought else beside,"
forgetful that if we have the fire of Love,
why worry about the sparks, and if we
have the perfect round, why trouble ourselves with the arc.

We always make the fatal mistake of
thinking that it is what we do that matters, when really what matters is what
we let God do to us. God sent the angel

to Mary, not to ask her to do something, but to let something be done.

Since God is a better artisan than you, the more you abandon yourself to Him, the happier He can make you. It is well to be a self-made man, but it is better to be a God-made man.

God will love you, of course, even though you do not love Him, but remember if you give Him only half your heart, He can make you only fifty percent happy. You have freedom only to give it away? To whom do you give yours? You give it either to the moods of the hour, to your egotism, to creatures or to God?

Do you know that if you give your freedom to God, in heaven you will have no freedom of choice, because once you possess the Perfect, there is nothing left to choose? And still you will be perfectly free, because you will be One with Him Whose Heart is Freedom and Love!

THE THIRD WORD

The Fellowship of Religion

CHAPTER III

THE THIRD WORD

The Fellowship of Religion

HAVE you ever said, in order to justify your selfishness, "After all, I have my own life to live?" The truth is you have not your own life to live, because you have to live it with everyone else. Religion is not what you do with your solitariness, but what you do with your relationships. You were born out of the womb of society, and hence the love of neighbor is inseparable from love of God. "If any man say: I love God, and hateth his brother; he is a liar. For he that loveth not his brother whom he seeth, how can he love God whom he seeth not?" (1 John 4:20)

As danger multiplies, human solidarity becomes more evident. Human beings are closer to one another morally in a bomb shelter or shell-hole than they are in a brokerage office or at a bridge table. As sorrow increases, a sense of unity deepens. It is, therefore, only natural to suspect that the peak of tragedy in the lives of our Divine Lord and His Mother on Calvary should best reveal the communal character of religion.

It is particularly interesting to note that the Word Our Lord spoke to His Mother from the Cross is prefaced by St. John, in His Gospel, speaking of the seamless garment which had been worn by our Blessed Lord and for which the soldiers were now shaking dice. "The soldiers therefore, when they had crucified him, took his garments, (and they made four parts, to every soldier a part) and also his coat. Now the coat was without seam, woven from the top throughout." (John 19:23)

Why, out of all the details of the Passion, should he suddenly begin thinking about a robe? Because it was woven by Mary's hands. It was such a beautiful robe that these hardened criminals refused to tear it apart. Custom gave them the right to the perquisites of those whom they crucified. But here the criminals refused to divide the spoils. They shook dice for it, so that the winner had the whole robe.

After having yielded up His garments to those who shook dice for them, He on the Cross now yields up her who wove the seamless garment. Our Blessed Lord looks down to the two most beloved creatures He has on earth: Mary and John. He speaks first to His Blessed Mother. He does not call her "Mother," but "Woman."

As St. Bernard so lovingly put it, if He had called her "Mother," she would have been just His Mother and no one else's. In order to indicate that she is now becoming the Mother of all men whom He redeems, He endows her with the title of universal motherhood: "Woman." Then indicating with a gesture of His head the presence of His beloved disciple, He added: "Behold thy son." He does not call him John, for if

He did, John would have been only the son of Zebedee; he left him unnamed that he might stand for all humanity.

Our Lord was equivalently saying to His Mother: "You already have one Son and I am He. You cannot have another. All the other sons will be in Me as the branches are in the vine. John is one in Me and I in him. Hence I say not: 'Behold another son!' but 'Behold Me in John and John in Me.'"

It was a kind of testament. At the Last Supper He willed to mankind His Body and Blood. "This is My Body! This is My Blood!" Now He was willing His Mother: "Behold thy Mother." Our Blessed Lord was here establishing a new relationship; a relationship by which His own Mother became the mother of all mankind, and we in turn became her children.

This new bond was not carnal, but spiritual. There are other ties than those of blood. Blood may be thicker than water, but Spirit is thicker than blood. All men, whatever be their color, race, blood, are one in the Spirit: "For whosoever shall do the will of my Father, that is in heaven, he is my brother, and sister, and mother." (Matt. 12:50)

Mary had seen God in Christ; now her Son was telling her to see her Christ in all Christians. She was never to love anyone else but Him, but He would now be in those whom He redeemed. The night before He had prayed that all men might be one in Him, as there is but one life for the Vine and its branches. Now He was making her the custodian not only of the Vine but also of the branches through time and eternity. She had given birth to the King; now she was begetting the Kingdom.

The very thought of this Bride of the Spirit becoming the Mother of humanity is overwhelming, not because God thought of it, but because we so seldom ever think of it. We have become so used to seeing the Madonna with the Child in Bethlehem that we forget that same Madonna is holding you and me at Calvary.

At the Manger, Christ was only a Babe; at Calvary, Christ was the head of re-deemed humanity. At Bethlehem, she was the mother of Christ; on Calvary, she be-came the Mother of Christians. In the stable, she brought forth her Son without pain and became the Mother of Joy; at the Cross, she brought us forth in pain and became the Queen of Martyrs. In neither case shall a woman forget the child of her womb.

When Mary heard Our Blessed Lord establish this new relationship, she remem-bered so well when this spiritual fellow-ship began. Her third word, as His, was about the relationship. It was a long time ago.

After the angel announced to her that she was to be the Mother of God, which alone would have bound her to all humanity, the angel added that her elder-ly cousin, Elizabeth, was now with child: "And behold thy cousin Elizabeth, she also hath conceived a son in her old age: and this is the sixth month with her that is called barren. Because no word shall be impossible with God. And Mary said: Behold the handmaid of the Lord: be it done to me according to thy word. And the angel departed from her.

"And Mary rising up in those days, went into the hill country with haste into a city of Juda. And she entered into the house of Zachary and saluted Elizabeth. And it came to pass that when Elizabeth heard the salutation of Mary, the infant leaped in her womb. And Elizabeth was filled with the Holy Ghost. And she cried out with a loud voice and said: Blessed art thou among women and blessed is the fruit of thy womb. And whence is this to me that the mother of my Lord should come to me? For behold as soon as the voice of thy salutation sounded in my ears, the infant in my womb leaped for joy. And blessed art thou that hast believed, because those things shall be accomplished that were spoken to thee by the Lord." (Luke 1:36-45)

It is rightly assumed that no one may more justly claim immunity from service to others than a woman bearing a child. If one adds to this, *noblesse oblige,* the fact that this Woman bear within herself the very Lord of the Universe, then of all creatures she might rightfully claim dispensation from social bonds and duties to neighbor. Women in that condition come not to minister but to be ministered unto.

Here we have the spectacle of the greatest of all women becoming the servant of others. Not standing on her dignity saying, "I am the Mother of God," but recognizing the need of her aged cousin, this pregnant Queen, instead of awaiting her hour in isolation *as* other women, mounts a donkey, makes a five day journey over hill country, and with such a consciousness of spiritual fellowship that she does it, in the language of Sacred Scripture, "with haste." (Luke 1:39)

Thirty-three years before Calvary,

Mary recognizes that her mission is to bring her Lord to humanity; and with such a holy impatience is she filled that she begins it before her Son has seen the light of day. I love to think of her on this journey as the first Christian Nurse whose service to neighbor is inseparable from bringing Christ into the life of her patient.

There is no record of the exact words that Mary spoke. The Evangelist merely tells us that she saluted Elizabeth. But notice that just as soon as she saluted her cousin, new relationships were immediately established. Elizabeth no longer addresses her as cousin. She says, "Whence is this to me, that the mother of my Lord should come to me?" (Luke 1:43)

Mary is now not just a relative, or another mother of another child. She is called the "Mother of God!" But that was not the end of the relationship. Elizabeth's own child in her womb, who was to be called later by the Child in Mary's womb "the greatest man ever born of woman," now stirs in his mother's womb; we might

almost say he danced to his birth in salutation to the King of Kings! Two unborn
children establish a relationship before
either had swung open the portals of flesh.

Notice how much our Blessed Lady is
made the link of bringing Christ to humanity. First of all, it was through her as
a Gate of Heaven that He walked into
this earth. It was in her as a Mirror of
Justice that He first saw with human eyes
the reflection of the world He had made.
It is in her as a kind of living ciborium
that He is carried to the First Communion
rail of her cousin's home, where an unborn
babe salutes Him as the Host who is to be
the Guest of the world. It is through her
intercession at Cana that He brings His
Divine Power to supply a human need.
And it is finally at the Cross that she who
gave Christ to the world, now receives
Him back again in us who have the high
and undeserved honor to call ourselves
Christian.

Because of this intimacy I wonder if
it is not true that as the world loses ven-

eration for Christ's mother, it loses also its adoration of Christ. Is it not true in earthly relationships that, as a so-called friend ignores your mother when he comes to your home, sooner or later he will ignore you? Conversely, as the world begins knocking at Mary's door, it will find that Our Lord Himself will answer.

If you have never before prayed to Mary, do so now. Can you not see that if Christ Himself willed to be physically formed in her for nine months and then be spiritually formed by her for thirty years, it is to her that we must go to learn how to have Christ formed in us? Only she who raised Christ can raise a Christian.

To develop that spiritual comradeship with Jesus and Mary, the Rosary is most effective. The word, Rosary, means a "garland of roses" culled from the Garden of Prayer. Each decade requires only between two and three minutes, thus the whole rosary requires only a little over ten minutes.

If you do not say it all at once and

on your knees, then say one decade when
you arise in the morning, another decade on your way to work; another decade
as you sweep the house or wait for your
check at the noon lunch hour; another
decade just before you go to bed; the
last decade you can say in bed just before
falling off to sleep.

When you are under twenty-five, you
have time for only one decade before falling to sleep; when you get to be forty,
you will have time for two; and when you
are sixty, you will have time for a dozen.

Because the "Hail Mary" is said many
times in the course of a Rosary, do not
think of it as a sterile repetition, because
each time it is said in a different setting
or scene as you meditate, for example, on
such mysteries as the Birth of Our Lord,
the Crucifixion, the Resurrection, etc. You
never thought as a child, when you told
your mother you loved her, that it had
the same meaning as it did the last time
you told her. Because the background of
the affection changed, its affirmation was

new. It is the same sun that rises each morning, but it makes a new day.

What are some of the advantages of the Rosary:

1. If you say the Rosary devoutly, and all that it implies, every day of your life, you will never lose your soul.

2. If you wish for peace in your heart and in your family and an abundance of heavenly gifts on your household, then assemble your family each night and say the Rosary.

3. If you are anxious to convert a soul to the fulness of God's Love and Life, teach that person to say the Rosary. That person will either stop saying the Rosary or he will receive the gift of Faith.

4. If a sufficient army of us said the Rosary every day, the Blessed Mother would now, as in the past, obtain from Her Divine Son the stilling of the present tempests, the defeat of the enemies of human civilization, and a real peace in the hearts of tired and straying men.

5. If the cooling of your charity has

made you unhappy on the inside and critical of others, then the Rosary, through meditation on Our Lord's great Love for you on the Cross and your Mother's affection for you on Calvary, will rekindle your love of God and of neighbor and restore you to a peace which surpasses all understanding.

Do not think that in honoring Our Lady with the Rosary you are neglecting Our Lord. Did you ever know anyone who ignored you by being kind to your mother? If Our Lord said to you "Behold, Thy Mother," it well behooves us to respect her whom Our Lord chose above all the creatures of earth. In any case remember, even though you wanted to, you could not stop with her. As Francis Thompson put it:

> The celestial Temptress play,
> And all mankind to bliss betray;
> With sacrosanct cajoleries
> And starry treachery of your eyes,
> Tempt us back to Paradise!

THE FOURTH WORD

Confidence in Victory

CHAPTER IV

THE FOURTH WORD

Confidence in Victory

PERHAPS at no time in modern history was there ever such a flight from life as at the present day. In much modern literature this is manifested either by a return to the primitive through sex, or through the subconscious.

In daily life, too, there is the flight from consciousness through alcoholism, or the flight from decision through indifference, or the flight from freedom by the denial of responsibility. All these are symptoms of despair. Many people as a result are cracking up, emotionally, mentally and morally. Our problem is not to diagnose the malady, but to heal it.

Is there another way out, even in these dark days? For an answer one must go back to the darkest day the world ever saw, the day when the sun hid its face at noon, as if ashamed to shed its light on the crime men committed at Calvary. It recalled the dark moment of the Old Law when the High Priest, clothed not in gorgeous golden robes, but in simple white, entered into the darkness of the Holy of Holies, to sprinkle it with blood in atonement for the sins of the people. The people could not see him, nor could they hear him. They only knew that his being there was a matter of supreme importance, for not until he emerged might they feel that the weight of their sins had been lifted.

One day that symbol became a reality as darkness spread over the earth, blurring three crosses silhouetted against a black horizon. The True High Priest, clothed in Innocence entered into that place where God had hidden Himself because of man's sins, to sprinkle the Holy of Holies with His own Blood in reparation for the sins of men. We see nothing; there is only an awful silence, a thick gloom, relieved by one cry, sent up from a broken heart of self-abasement: "My God, My God, Why hast thou forsaken me?" (Mark 15:34)

These words were the first words of the prophetic Psalm 21, written 1000 years before this black day. Though the Psalm begins with sadness, it ends with joy, victory, and the assurance of spiritual sovereignty over the earth.

First there is sorrow:

"O God, my God, look upon me: Why hast thou forsaken me?

"But I am a worm and no man: the reproach of men and the outcast of the people.

"All they that saw me have laughed me to scorn: they have spoken with the lips and wagged the head.

"He hoped in the Lord, let him deliver him: let him save him, seeing he delighteth in him.

"They have dug my hands and feet. They have numbered all my bones.

"And they have looked and stared upon

me. They parted my garments amongst them: and upon my vesture they cast lots."

Then comes the promise of victory:

"Ye that fear the Lord, praise him: all ye the seed of Jacob, glorify him.

"Let all the seed of Israel fear him: because he hath not slighted nor despised the supplication of the poor man.

"Neither hath he turned away his face from me: and when I cried to him he heard me.

"The poor shall eat and shall be filled: and they shall praise the Lord that seek him: their hearts shall live for ever and ever.

"All the ends of the earth shall remember, and shall be converted to the Lord: And all the kindreds of the Gentiles shall adore in his sight.

"For the kingdom is the Lord's; and he shall have dominion over the nations." (Ps. 21:1-29)

Mary standing at the foot of the Cross, knew her scriptures well. When she heard

Our Lord begin Psalm 21 it reminded her of a song that she sang too. It was her fourth word which she chanted in the home of Elizabeth, the greatest song ever written, "The Magnificat": "My soul doth magnify my Lord." It contains very much the same sentiments of Psalm 21, namely, the assurance of victory.

"And Mary said: My soul doth magnify the Lord. And my spirit hath rejoiced in God my Saviour. Because he hath regarded the humility of his handmaid: for behold from henceforth all generations shall call me blessed. Because he that is mighty hath done great things to me: and holy is his name. And his mercy is from generation unto generations, to them that fear him. He hath shewed might in his arm: he hath scattered the proud in the conceit of their heart. He hath put down the mighty from their seat and hath exalted the humble. He hath filled the hungry with good things: and the rich he hath sent empty away. He hath received Israel his servant, being mindful of his mercy. As he spoke to our fathers: to Abraham and to his seed for ever." (Luke 1:46-55)

There is something common to both these songs: both were spoken before there was any assurance of victory. In His fourth word from the Cross, the suffering figure looks forward through the darkness to the triumph of the Resurrection, and His spiritual dominion over the earth. In her fourth word, the Woman, nine months before her child is born, looks down the long procession of the coming ages, and proclaims that when the world's great women like Livia, Julia and Octavia shall have been forgotten, the ordinary law of human oblivion will be suspended in her favor, because she is the Mother of Him Whose Name is Holy, and Whose Cross is the Redemption of men.

How hopeless from a human point of view was the prospect of a Man of the Cross crying to God in darkness, ever exercising dominion over the earth that rejected Him! How hopeless from a human point of view was the prospect of an insignificant village maiden begetting a Son Who would be the Supreme Revolutionist of the centuries, exalting the poor to the family of the Godhead!

Both were really words of triumph, one of Victory before the battle was over, one of Overlordship before the Lord was born. To both Jesus and Mary, there were treasures in darkness, whether the darkness be on a black hill or in a dark womb.

Are you in the valley of despair? Then learn that the Gospel of Christ can be heard as Good News even by those whose life has been shattered by Bad News, for only those who walk in darkness ever see the stars.

All trusting implies something you cannot see. If you could see, there would be no occasion for trust. When you say you trust a man only insofar as you can see him, you do not trust him at all. Now to trust God means to hold fast to the truth that His purposes are good and holy, not because you see them, but in spite of appearances to the contrary.

The reason, therefore, why some souls emerge purified from catastrophe, while other souls come out worse, is because the first had One in Whom they could trust and the second had none but themselves. The atheist, therefore, is properly defined as the person who has no invisible means of support.

Have you ever noticed, as you talk to your fellowmen, the difference in the re-action to crisis on the part of those who have faith in God and His purposes and of those who have not? The man without faith was generally greatly surprised at the dark turn of events with two world wars in twenty-one years, the resurgence of barbarism and the abandonment of moral principles. But the man with faith in God was not so surprised. The sum came out just as he had expected; chaos was in the cards though they had not yet been dealt, for he knew that "unless the

Lord build the house, they labour in vain that build it." (Ps. 126:1)

Have you also observed that the man without faith, finding his world of "progress" becoming so unprogressive, often reacted by blaming religion, by criticizing the Church, and even by blaspheming God for not stopping the war? Such egotists have some sense of justice, and since they refuse to blame themselves, then must find a scapegoat.

But the man with faith, in the midst of taunts like that which came from the haughty monarch, "Who is the God that shall deliver you out of my hand," (Daniel 3:15) answers as did the three youths in the fiery furnace: "For behold our God, whom we worship, is able to save us from the furnace of burning fire and to deliver us out of thy hands, O king. But if he will not, be it known to thee, O king, that we will not worship thy gods nor adore the golden statue which thou hast set up." (Daniel 3:17-18) "Although he should kill me, I will trust in him." (Job 13:15)

To bring out this difference between those who can call on God in darkness and those who do not, let us set in contrast a typical modern without faith, and a saint. As an example of the first, take H. G. Wells who for decades hoped that "man with his feet on earth, would one day have hands reaching among the stars."

When darkness fell over the earth in these last few years, he turned to pessimism. "There is no reason whatever to believe that the order of nature has any greater bias in favor of man than it had in favor of the ichthyosaur. In spite of all my disposition to a brave looking optimism, I perceive that now the universe is bored with him, is turning a hard face to him, and I see him being carried less and less intelligently, and more and more rapidly . . . along the stream of fate to degradation, suffering, and death."

Now hear St. Paul, who already had been persecuted, and who knew that the tyrant who held the sword would one day draw it across his neck:

"We are reviled: and we bless. We are persecuted: and we suffer it.

"We are blasphemed: and we entreat. We are made as the refuse of this world." (I Cor. 4:12-13)

"Who then shall separate us from the love of Christ? Shall tribulation? Or distress? Or famine? Or nakedness? Or danger? Or persecution? Or the sword?

"For I am sure that neither death, nor life, nor Angels, nor principalities, nor powers, nor things present, nor things to come, nor might.

"Nor height, nor depth, nor any other creature, shall be able to separate us from the love of God which is in Christ Jesus our Lord." (Romans 8:35, 38-39)

Take another comparison in time of trouble. Hear Bertrand Russell, a typical modern without faith in God. What is his hope for man?

"Man's origin, his growth, his hopes, fears, his loves, and beliefs, are but the outcome of accidental collocation of atoms. That no fire, no heroism, no intensity of thought and feeling, can preserve the individual beyond the grave; that all the labour of the ages, all devotion, all the inspiration, all the noonday brightness of human genius are destined to extinction, and that the whole temple of Man's achievement must be buried beneath the debris of a universe in ruins. Only on the firm foundation of unyielding despair can the soul's habitation be safely built."

Now turn to St. Augustine who lived in a world of despair when the Roman Empire that had survived for centuries fell, even as Satan fell from heaven, to the barbarians from the North.

"God, Who is not the Author of evil, but Who allowest it to exist in order to prevent greater evil.

"God Who art loved, knowingly or unknowingly, by everything that is capable of loving.

"God, in Whom all things are, yet Who receivest from the ignominy of creatures, no ignominy, from their malice, no malice, from their errors, no errors.

"God, from Whom to turn is to fall, towards Whom to turn, is to rise again, in Whom to dwell, is to find firm support; from Whom to depart is to die, to return to Whom, is to be restored to life, to dwell in Whom, is to live.

"God, Whom to forsake is the same as to perish, Whom to search for is the same as to love, Whom to see is the same as to possess.

"God, towards Whom faith urges, hope raises us, charity unites us. God, through Whom we triumph over our enemy.

"Thee I invoke.

"To Thee I address my prayers."

You see the difference! Now choose! Will you slip down into abysmal despair, or will you, like Christ in a blackness at high noon, and like Mary ere her Tree of Life had seen the earth, trust in God, His Mercy and His Victory?

If you are unhappy, or sad, or despondent, it is basically for only one reason: you have refused to respond to Love's plea: "Come to me, all you that labour and are burdened, and I will refresh you. Take up my yoke upon you and learn of me, because I am meek, and humble of heart: and you shall find rest to your souls." (Matt. 11:28-29) Everywhere else but in Him, the liberation promised is either armed or forced, and that can mean slavery. Only *nailed* love is free. Unnailed and uncrucified love can compel. Hands pinioned to a wooden beam cannot compel, nor can a lifted Host and an elevated Chalice constrain, but they can beckon and solicit.

That kind of love gives you these three suggestions for living in troubled times:

1) Never forget that there are only two philosophies to rule your life: the one of the Cross, which starts with the fast and ends with the feast. The other of Satan, which starts with the feast and ends with the headache. Unless there is the Cross, there will never be the empty

tomb; unless there is faith in darkness, there will never be vision in light; unless there is a Good Friday, there will never be an Easter Sunday. In the beautiful assurance of our Lord: "Amen, amen, I say to you, that you shall lament and weep, but the world shall rejoice: and you shall be made sorrowful, but your sorrow shall be turned into joy." (John 16:20)

2) When bereavement comes, and when the "slings and arrows of outrageous fortune" strike, when like Simon of Cyrene a cross is laid on your reluctant shoulders, take that Cross to daily Mass and say to our Lord at the moment of consecration: "As Thou my Saviour in love for me dost say: 'This is My Body! This is My Blood!' so I say to Thee: 'This is my body! Take it. This is my blood! Take it. They are yours. I care not if the accidents or species of my life remain, with my daily work, my routine duties. But all that I am substantially, take, consecrate, ennoble, spiritualize; turn my cross into

a Crucifix, so that I am no longer mine, but Thine, O Love Divine!' "

3) Think not of Almighty God as a kind of absentee landlord with whom you hardly dare to be familiar, or to whom you go to fix your leaks, or to get yourself out of a mess. Think neither of God as an insurance agent, who can protect you against loss by fire. Approach him not timidly as a stenographer might approach her boss for a raise, fearful, half believing that you will never receive what you seek. Do not fear Him with a servile fear, for God is more patient with you than you are with yourself. Would you for example, be as patient with the wicked world today as He is? Would you even be as patient with anyone else who had the same faults as you? Rather approach Him in full confidence and even with the boldness of a loving child who has a right to ask a Father for favors.

Though He may not grant all your wants, be sure that, in a certain sense, there is no unanswered prayer. A child asks his father for something that may not be good for him, e.g. a gun. The father, while refusing, will pick up the child in his arms to console him, giving the response of love, even in the denial of a request. As the child forgets in that embrace that he ever asked a favor, so in praying you forget what you wanted by receiving what you needed—a return of love. Do not forget either, that there are not two kinds of answers to prayer, but three: One is "Yes." Another is "No." The third is "Wait."

You will find that, as you pray, the nature of your requests will change. You will ask less and less things for yourself, and more and more for His Love. Is it not true in human relationships that the more you love someone, the more you seek to give and the less you desire to receive? The deepest love never says: "Give me," but it does say: "Make me." You probably think that if Our Lord came into your room some night as you were praying, you would ask Him favors, or present your difficulties, or say: "When will the war end?" or "Should I buy General Motors stock?" or "Give me a million."

No! You would throw yourself on your knees and kiss the hem of His garment. And the moment He laid His hands on your head, you would feel such a peace and trust and confidence—even in darkness—that you would not even remember you had questions to ask, or favors to beg. You would consider them a kind of desecration. You would want only to look into His face, and you would be in a world which only lovers know. That would be the only Heaven you wanted!

THE FIFTH WORD

Religion is a Quest

CHAPTER V

THE FIFTH WORD

Religion is a Quest

EVERY human heart in the world without exception is on the quest of God. Not everyone may be conscious of it; but they are conscious of their desire for happiness which some in ignorance, perversity, or weakness, identify with the tinsel and baubles of earth. It is as natural for the soul to want God as for the body to want food or drink. It was natural for the prodigal son to be hungry; it was unnatural to live on husks. It is natural to want God; it is unnatural to satisfy that want with false gods.

On the other hand, not only is the soul on the quest of God, but God is on the quest of the soul, inviting everyone to His Banquet of Love. But since love is free, His invitation is rejected in the Gospel language either because they have just married, or because they have bought a farm, or because they must try a yoke of oxen.

This double quest of the Creator for the creature, and the creature for the Creator, is revealed in the Fifth Word of our Lord from the Cross, and the Fifth Word of our Lady, pronounced when her Son was only twelve years of age.

One day Our Blessed Lord said to the multitude: "If any man thirst, let him come to me and drink." (John 7:37) But on the Cross, He, from whose finger-tips toppled planets and worlds, He Who filled the valleys with the song of a thousand fountains now cries, not to God, but to man: "I thirst." (John 19:28) The physical pain of being nailed to a cross, lingering for hours without food or drink beneath an Oriental sun, the parched dryness that came from loss of blood, now expresses itself not in peevish impatience but in a simple declaration of thirst.

There is nothing in the whole story of

the Crucifixion which makes our Lord
seem so human as this one Word. And yet
that thirst could not have been only physical, for the Gospel tells us, that He said it
in order that the Scriptures might be ful-
filled. It, therefore, was spiritual as well
as physical. God was on the quest of souls,
trusting that one of the trivial ministra-
tions of life, the offering of a cup in His
name, might bring the offerer within the
sweet radiance of His Grace. The Shepherd was still out after the sheep, at the
moment when He was giving His Life for
the flock!

Mary standing in the shadow of her
Son's hard death-bed heard His Word and
knew that it was more than a plea for re-
lief. She remembered so well the Psalm
from which it was taken. Hearing it, she
was reminded of the time she thirsted,
too. It was just when her little Son reached
the legal age of twelve. During the Feast
of the unleavened bread, instituted in re-
membrance of the Exodus from Egypt,
Mary and Joseph joined the pilgrimage

to the Holy City. After seven days, according to custom, the multitude departed
in the afternoon, the men leaving by one
gate, the women by another, to reunite
at the halting place of the first night.
Joseph and Mary left, each thinking the
Child was with the other, only to discover
at nightfall that He was not with either.

If the trumpets of doom had sounded,
their hearts would have been less heavy.
For three days they flushed the hills and
the caravans, and on the third day they
found Him. We know not where He was
during those three days. We can only
guess. Perhaps He was visiting Gethsemani where His Blood twenty-one years
later would crimson the olive roots; perhaps He stood on Calvary's hill and saw
this sad hour. In any case, on the third
day they found Him in the temple, teach-
ing the doctors of the law. Mary said:
"Son, why hast thou done so to us? Behold thy father and I have sought Thee
sorrowing." (Luke 2:48) In a land where
women were reticent, where men were

always masters, it was not Joseph who spoke. It was Mary. Mary was the mother, Joseph was the foster-father.

When Abraham drew near to God a "great and darksome horror seized upon him" (Gen. 15:12), and when the Lord appeared, "Abraham fell flat on his face." (Gen. 17:3) When Jacob saw the Lord, he trembled saying: "How terrible is this place." (Gen. 28:17) When Moses came in the presence of God, "Moses hid his face." (Ex. 3:6) And yet here, a woman addresses Him Who is the Author of Life, through whom all things were made and without Whom nothing is made, as *"Son."* She called Him that by right and not by privilege. That one word shows the intimate relationship between the two, and it was probably her usual way of addressing Him in Nazareth.

Here was a creature on the quest of God. As our Blessed Lord's thirst on the Cross revealed the Creator in search of man, Mary's words revealed its complementary truth that the creature is in search of God.

If each is seeking for the other, why do they not find? God does not always find man because man is free, and like Adam man can hide from God. Like a child who hides from his mother when he does something wrong, so does man turn from God when he sins. God then always seems "so far away;" but the truth is, it is man who is "far away." Sin creates a distance. Respecting human freedom, God calls, but He does not force. "I thirst" is the language of liberty.

God is closer to us than we suspect as Paul told the Athenians. He may be somewhat disguised and appear like a gardener as He did to Mary Magdalen, or like a chance acquaintance on a roadway, as He did to the disciples of Emmaus. What must have been the chagrin, therefore, of the inn-keepers of Bethlehem when they discovered that they had refused hospitality to the Mother of Our Lord! If they ever met Our Blessed Mother later on, they probably chided her saying: "Why did you not tell us that you were the Mother of Jesus?" If any of the bystanders at the Crucifixion within the next forty days saw the Risen and Glorified Saviour, how they must have mourned in their hearts, saying: "If I had only known, it was You Who asked for a drink."

Why is it that in religion we want a proof and a manifestation so strong that it will overwhelm our reason and destroy our freedom? That God will never grant! On man's side the regret will continue even until Judgment! When Christ shall say: "I was thirsty and you gave me not to drink." (Matt. 25:42)

"The angels keep their ancient places;—
Turn but a stone, and start a wing!
'Tis ye, 'tis your estranged faces,
That miss the many-splendoured thing."

From the Fifth Word of Jesus and Mary there emerges the lesson that the apostolate of religion should start with the assumption that everyone wants God. Bigots? Do they want Our Lord and His Church? Certainly they think more about the Church than some who belong to it. Be not too hard on them.

They do not really hate the Church. They hate only what they mistakenly believe to be the Church. If I had heard the same lies about the Church they have heard, and if I had been taught the same historical perversions as they, with my own peculiar character and temperament, I would hate the Church ten times more than they do. At least they have some zeal and some fire. It may be misdirected, but with God's grace it can be channeled into love as well as hate.

These souls who peddle anti-religion tracts or anti-Catholic publications are to be regarded in exactly the same light as St. Paul before his conversion. And as he preached and lectured against the Church, after assisting at the killing of the most brilliant of the early Churchmen, St. Stephen, there were many believers who despaired. Prayers were multiplied to God: "Send someone to refute Paul." And God heard their prayers. God sent Paul to answer Paul. A bigot made the best Apostle.

In my radio audience a few years ago was a young woman who used to sit before the radio and ridicule and scoff and wise-crack at every word. She is now enjoying the fulness of Faith and the Sacraments. In another town was a man who used to make records of these broadcasts, then take them to a nearby convent, and play them for the sisters, who had no radio. But he mitigated this act of kindness by making a running commentary of ridicule while the record played. He recently built the new Sisters' school in that city. Every-one is on the quest of God, and if the soul gives God a chance, God will win.

God is thirsting, too, for those who have lost the Faith. The position of the fallen-away Catholic is rather unique. The se-riousness of his fall is to be measured by the heights from which he fell. His reac-

tion to the Church is either hate or argu-
ment. In both cases he bears witness to the
Divinity of the Church. The hate is his
vain attempt to despise. Since his conscience which was informed by the Spirit
in the Church will not let him alone, he
will not let the Church alone.

But the general truth still holds true:
assume that he is on the quest of the
Divine, otherwise he would not think so
much about it. Hence never, never, never
argue with a fallen away Catholic. He may
tell you, for example, that he left because
he could not believe in Confession. Do not
believe it. He left because he refused in
his pride to confess his sins. He wants to
argue to salve his conscience; but he needs
absolution to heal it. Like the woman at
the well, who had five husbands, he wants
to keep religion in the realm of the specu-
lative. What he needs is to have it brought
down in the realm of the moral, as our
Blessed Lord did for that woman. His
difficulty is not with the Creed: it is with

the commandments. Having tasted the best, he is miserable without it.

We do not help him by telling him why the road he took was wrong. He knows it. He even knows the right road. We can help him best, like the father of the prodigal, by going out on the road to meet him and make the return journey easy, for every prodigal wants to get back home.

Sinners, too, want God. That is to say, conscious sinners. One need hardly ever tell such a sinner how wicked he is. He knows it a thousand times better than you. His conscience has pointed an accusing finger at him in his sleep; his fears have emblazoned his sins on his mind; his neurosis, anxieties and unhappiness have been like trumpets of his inner death.

This consciousness of sin is not yet conversion, for up to this point a soul may be repenting like Judas, only to itself. One can be mad at oneself for playing the fool, or be ashamed at one's misdeeds, or be sad at being discovered, but there is no true repentance without a turning to God. The consciousness of sin creates the vacuum; grace alone can fill it.

You say: "I am a sinner. I will not be heard." If God will not hear a sinner, why did He praise the publican in the rear of the temple, who struck his breast saying: "O God, be merciful to me a sinner." (Luke 18:13) There were two sinners on Calvary on either side of our Lord. One was saved because he asked to be saved. Did not our Divine Saviour say: "Come to Me, all you that labor and are burdened" (Matt. 11:28)—and who is more heavily burdened than a sinner? Unlike all other religions, Christianity starts with the sinner. In a certain sense, it begins with human hopelessness. You have to be good to enter most other religions; you become a Christian on the assumption that you are not good.

God will find you, if your will does not refuse to be found. Hence, avoid those selfish and petty acts which may deaden and stunt you in the one great moment when surrender to the Divine Will can bring peace. In that case we become like the cobbler of Charles Dickens. For years he had been a prisoner in the Bastille, where he cobbled shoes. He became so enamored of the walls, the darkness, and the task's monotony, that when he was liberated, he built a cell at the center of his English home, and on days when skies were clear and birds were singing, the taps of the cobbler in the dark could still be heard. So men by habitual residence in imprisoning moods render themselves incapable of living in wider horizons, the great hopes and faith of religion.

Stunt not your spiritual life by looking for faults. You do not say Shakespeare cannot write because you heard a poor actor butcher the soliloquy of Hamlet; you do not reject the beauty of music because you hear an occasional moaner or groaner on the radio; you do not disbelieve in medicine because your doctor has a cold.

Give God a chance. The prolongation of His Incarnate Life in the Church is an offer, not a demand. It is a gift, not a bargain. You can never deserve it, but you can receive it. God is on the quest of your soul. Whether you will know peace depends on your own will. "If any man will do the will of him, he shall know of the doctrine, whether it be of God, or whether I speak of myself." (John 7:17)

THE SIXTH WORD

The Hour

CHAPTER VI

THE SIXTH WORD

The Hour

THE MOST current philosophy of life to-day is self-expressionism: "Let yourself go;" "Do whatever you please." Any suggestion of restraining errant impulses is called a masochistic survival of the dark ages. The truth is that the only really self-expressive people in the world are in the insane asylum. They have absolutely no inhibitions, no conventions and no codes. They are as self-expressive as hell, i.e., in complete disorder.

Self-expressive lives in this sense are self-destructive. Yet there is a way to be truly self-expressive in the sense of self-perfection. But this is impossible without sacrifice. Incompleteness is always the lot of the undisciplined. To understand this lesson we turn to Calvary.

When Our Blessed Lord uttered His Fifth Word to the Cross, "I Thirst," (John 19:28) a soldier nearby—soldiers are always mentioned kindly in the Scripture—put some wine on a hyssop, and placing it at the end of a long reed reached it to the mouth of Our Blessed Lord, who tasted the wine. The Evangelist adds, "Jesus therefore, when he had taken the vinegar, said: 'It is consummated.'" (John 19:30)

Three times this word is used in Sacred Scripture. At the beginning of the world, at the end, and in between. In creation, the Heavens and earth are described as "finished." At the end of the world, a Great Voice is heard coming out of the Temple saying: "It is finished." And now, from the Cross, it is heard again. The word does not mean, "Thank God, it is over." It means it is perfected, the debt had been paid, the work that He had come to do had been completed.

When Mary at the foot of the Cross saw that soldier offer Him wine and heard

Him say, "It is consummated," she thought of the moment when it all began. There was wine there too, but not enough. It was the marriage feast of Cana. When in the course of the banquet the wine gave out, the first to observe the lack of wine was not the steward. It was Our Blessed Mother. She notes human needs even before those commissioned to supply them.

Our Blessed Mother said to Our Lord a simple prayer: "They have no wine." (John 2:3) That was all. And her Son answered: "Woman." He did not call her Mother. "Woman, what is that to me and to thee? My hour is not yet come." (John 2:4) Why "Woman"? He was equivalently saying to her: "Mary, you are My Mother. You are asking Me to begin My public life, to declare Myself the Messiah, the Son of God, by working My first miracle. The moment I do that you cease to be just My Mother. As I reveal myself as Redeemer, you become in a certain sense a co-redemptrix, the Mother of all men. That is why I address you by the title of universal Motherhood: 'Woman.' It will be the beginning of your womanhood."

But what did He mean by saying: "My hour is not yet come?" Our Blessed Lord used that word "hour" often in relation to His Passion and Death. When, for example, His enemies took up stones to throw at Him in the temple, the Evangelist says, "His hour was not yet come." (John 7:30) The night of the Last Supper, He prayed: "Father, the hour is come. Glorify thy Son, that thy Son may glorify thee." (John 17:1) Then when Judas came out into the Garden, Our Blessed Lord said: "This is your hour." (Luke 22:53) The Hour meant the Cross.

The working of His first miracle was the beginning of the hour. His sixth word from the Cross was the end of that hour. The Passion was finished. The water had been changed into wine; the wine into blood. It is perfected. The work is done.

From these words the lesson emerges

that, between the beginning of our as-
signed duties and their completion and
perfection, there intervenes an "hour," or
a moment of mortification, sacrifice and
death. No life is ever finished without it.
Between the Cana when we launch the
vocation of our lives, and that moment
of triumph when we can say we succeeded,
there must come the interval of the Cross.

Our Lord could have had no other mo-
tive in asking us to take up our cross daily
than to perfect ourselves. It was almost
like saying, between the day you begin to
be a concert pianist and the day you
triumph in concert work, there must come
the "hour" of hard study, dull exercises
and painful addiction to work.

It is very likely that the reason for the
answer Our Lord gave the Greeks when
they visited Him: "Unless the grain of
wheat falling into the ground die, itself
remaineth alone. But if it die, it bringeth
forth much fruit,"—was to remind them
that death is a condition of life. Athens
conceivably might have made Him a

teacher, but Jerusalem with its Hour would make Him a Redeemer.

The Christ Who is our Head is not a Christ unscarred, but a Christ slain and risen and bearing in His glorified Body the marks of "the Hour" on hands and feet and side. As St. Paul says: "And they that are Christ's have crucified their flesh, with the vices and concupiscences." (Gal. 5:24)

Short of this self-discipline by which we humble our pride, restrain our selfishness, our lives are unfinished and incomplete. Most lives are frustrated because they have left out the Cross. They think the endless Day of Eternity can be won without the Crucial Hour of Calvary. Nature abhors incompleteness. Cut off the leg of a salamander and it will grow another. The impulses we deny in our waking life are often completed in our dreams. Our mutilated souls in one way or another are trying to complete their incompleteness and to perfect their imperfection.

In the spiritual life this is a conscious, deliberate process: the application of the

"Hour" of Christ's Passion to ourselves
that we may share in His Resurrection.
"That I may know him and the power
of his resurrection and the fellowship of
his sufferings: being made conformable to
His death." (Phil. 3:10)

Our Lord, after rising from the tomb,
told the disciples on the way to Emmaus
that "the Hour" was the condition of His
glory. "O foolish and slow of heart to
believe in all things which the prophets
have spoken. Ought not Christ to have
suffered these things and so to enter his
glory?" (Luke 24:25, 26) Without some
systematic detachment on our part, therefore, it is impossible to advance in charity.

The finished man or the perfected man
is the non-attached man, non-attached to a
craving for power, publicity and possessions; non-attached to anger, ambition and
avarice; non-attached to selfish desires,
lusts and bodily sensations. The practice
of non-attachment to the things which
stunt our soul is one of the things meant
by "the Hour." It is a going "against the

grain;" a being on God's side even against oneself, a renouncement for the sake of recovery.

By what signs will you know whether your life is unfinished? Among others we mention these: First, the habit of criticism is the best indication of an incomplete life. Our sense of justice is so keen and deep, that we do not have it ourselves, we compensate for the lack by trying to make everyone else just. Criticism of others is thus an oblique form of self-commendation. We think we make the picture hang straight on our wall by telling our neighbors that all his pictures are crooked. Like the lark who flutters with great agitation over her nest, we exhibit most flagrantly the very things we seek to hide.

When you say of another's failing: "That is one thing I can not stand," you reveal the very thing to which you are most unconsciously inclined. We personalize and objectify our unrecognized failings by talking of the failings of others. We hate in others the sins to which we are most likely to be addicted. When Our Lord said "Judge not, that you may not be judged," (Matthew 7:1) He also meant, that you are judged by your judgment of others! You have given yourself away! You are trying to make up for not having the "Hour" by giving others a miserable day.

Another proof of incompleteness is revealed in criticism of religion either explicit or implicit. If you are a rationalist and regard faith as a superstition, you probably are very fond of ghost stories. You complete your incompleteness by a flight into the incredulous. If you regard all the mysteries of religion as so much worthless superstition, why do you read so many detective stories? You are filling up your need of heavenly mystery with murder mystery.

Why is it that the impure like to read books attacking the purity of others. Why are those who are notoriously undisciplined and unmoral also most contemptuous of religion and morality? They are trying to solace their own unhappy lives by pulling the happy down to their own abysmal depths. They erroneously believe that Bibles and religions, Churches and priests have in some way foisted the distinction between right and wrong in the world, and that if they would be done away with, they could go on sinning with impunity. They measure progress by the height of the pile of discarded moral truths.

A third mark of incompleteness is in a state of continual self-reference. The egocentric is always frustrated, simply because the condition of self-perfection is self-surrender. There must be a willingness to die to the lower part of self, before there can be a birth to the nobler. That is what Our Lord meant when He said: "For he that will save his life shall lose it; and he that shall lose his life for My sake shall find it." (Matt. 16:25)

Many married women who have deliberately spurned the "hour" of child-bearing are unhappy and frustrated. They never discovered the joys of marriage because they refused to surrender to the obligation of their state. In saving themselves, they lost themselves! It takes three to make love, not two: you and you and God. Without God people only succeed in bringing out the worst in each other. Lovers who have nothing else to do but love one another, soon find there is nothing else. Without a central loyalty life is unfinished.

The youth of America remain juvenile longer than in any other country of the world! The reason is, that so-called "progressive" education by neglecting self-discipline in favor of unbounded self-expression has denied them the one thing that would make them really progressive. To leave out the "hour" of self-renunciation is to make impossible the day of self-development.

It is only by dying to our lower self, that we live to the higher: it is only by surrendering that we control: it is only by crushing our egotism that we can develop our personality. How does the plant get its power to develop? By being unresponsive and unrelated to others, or by surrendering and adjusting itself to its environment that it may survive? How can we enjoy the swim except by surviving the shock of the first cold plunge; how can we enjoy the classics except after the dull routine of grammar? How can we live to the higher life of God unless we make ourselves receptive by self-denial?

Once you have surrendered yourself you make yourself receptive. In receiving from God you are perfected and completed. It is a law of nature and grace that only those who give, will ever receive. The Sea of Galilee is fresh and blue and gives life to all the living things within its sunlit waters—not because it receives waters, but because it gives them. The Dead Sea, on the contrary, is dead, simply because it has no outlet. It does not give and, therefore, it never receives. No fish can live in its waters, no beast can thrive upon its shores. Not having had its Calvary of surrender, it never has its Pentecost of Life and Power.

If nothing pleases you, it is because you do not please yourself. If you rarely find a person or thing you like, it is because you do not like yourself. Life does not allow egocentricity to establish its own order, for to life selfishness is disorder. But how shall this disordered self be oriented to others except by discipline? That is why in the center of the Kingdom of God there is a Cross.

THE SEVENTH WORD

The Purpose of Life

CHAPTER VII

THE SEVENTH WORD

The Purpose of Life

PROBABLY the word most often used in the contemporary scene is the word *Freedom*. If the sick talk most about health, because health is endangered, may it be that the modern talk about freedom means that we are in danger of losing it? It is indeed possible that while we fight to keep our enemies from binding chains to our feet, we become our own enemy by binding chains to our souls.

What I am trying to say is there are two kinds of freedom; a freedom *from* something, and a freedom *for* something; an external freedom from restraints, and an internal freedom of perfection; a freedom to choose evil and a freedom to possess the good.

This inner freedom the typical modern

man does not want, because it implies responsibility and, therefore, is a burden—the awful burden of answering, what is the purpose of your life? That is why theories which deny man's inner freedom are so popular today, e.g., Marxism, which destroys freedom in terms of historical determination; Freudianism, which dissolves freedom in the determination of the subconscious and the erotic; totalitarianism, which drowns individual freedom in the totality.

The root of all our trouble is that freedom for God and in God has been interpreted as freedom from God. Freedom is ours to give away. Each of us reveals what we believe to be the purpose of life by the way we use that freedom. For those who would know the supreme purpose of freedom, turn to the life of our Lord and our Lady.

The first word Our Lord is recorded as speaking in the Scripture is at the age of twelve: "I must be about my father's business." (Luke 2:49) During His public life, He re-affirmed His obedience to His Father: "I do always the things that please him." (John 8:29) Now on the Cross, when He goes out to meet death, and freely surrenders His life, His last words are: "Father, into thy hands I commend my spirit." (Luke 23:46) The last words of other men are spoken in whispers, but He spoke these words in a loud voice.

Death, therefore, did not come to Him; He went to death. No one took His Life away; He laid it down of Himself. He was strong enough to live, but He died by an act of will. This was not an emphasis on dying, but an affirmation of uninterrupted Divine Life. It was the beginning of His return to the glory which He had with the Father before the foundations of the world were laid.

"Father"—note the word of External Parenthood. He did not say "Our Father" as we do, for the Father was not His and ours in the same way. He

is the natural Son of the Father; we are
only the adopted sons.

"Into Thy Hands"—These were the
hands the prophet called "good;" the
hands that guided Israel to its historical
fulfillment; the hands that provided
good things even for the birds of the
air and the grass of the field.

"I commend my Spirit"—Surrender! Con-
secration. Life is a cycle. We come from
God and we go back again to God.
Hence the purpose of living is to do
God's Will.

When Our Blessed Mother saw Him
bow His head and deliver His spirit, she
remembered that last Word that she ever
is recorded to have spoken in Scripture.
It was to the wine steward at the marriage
feast of Cana: "Whatsoever He shall say
to you, do ye." (John 2:5) What a beautiful valedictory! They are the most magnificent words that ever came from the
lips of a woman: "Whatsoever He shall
say to you, do ye." At the Transfiguration

the Heavenly Father spoke from the Heavens and said: "This is my beloved Son . . . Hear ye him." (Matt. 17:5) Now our Blessed Mother speaks and says, "Do His Will."

The sweet relationship of three decades in Nazareth now draws to a close and Mary is about to give Emmanuel to us all, and she does it by pointing out to us the one and only way of salvation: complete consecration to her Divine Son. Nowhere in the Scripture is it ever said that Mary loved her Son. Words do not prove love. But that love is hidden under the submission of her mind to Him and her final injunction to us: "Whatsoever He shall say to you, do ye."

Both the last recorded word of Jesus and the last recorded word of Mary were words of surrender: Jesus surrendered Himself to the Father; Mary asked us to surrender ourselves to the Son. This is the law of the universe. "For all are yours: And you are Christ's. And Christ is God's." (I Cor. 3:22-23)

Now face the problem squarely: What do you do with your freedom? You can do three things with it:

1) Keep it for your selfish desires.
2) Break it up into tiny little areas of trivial allegiance or passing fancies.
3) Surrender it to God.

1) If you keep freedom only for yourself, then because it is arbitrary and without standards, you will find it deteriorating into a defiant self-affirmation. Once all things become allowable, simply because you desire them, you become the slave of your choices. If your self-will decides to drink as much as you please, you soon find not only that you are no longer free not to drink, but that you belong to drink and not drink to you. Boundless liberty is boundless tyranny. This is what Our Lord meant when He said: "Whosoever committeth sin is the servant of sin." (John 8:34)

2) The second way out is to become a dilettante, by using your freedom like a

humming bird, hovering first over this
flower, then over that, but living for none
and dying without any. You desire nothing with all your heart, because your heart
is broken into a thousand pieces. You thus
become divided against yourself; a civil
war wages within you, because you swim
in contradictory currents.

You change your likes and desires when
dissatisfied but you never change yourself. You are then very much like the man
who complained to the cook at breakfast
that the egg was not fresh and asked her
to bring another. She brought in an egg
a minute later, but when he got to the
bottom of it, he found it was the same
old egg turned upside down. So it is always the same self; what has changed is
the desire, not the soul. In that case, even
your interest in others is not real.

In your more honest moments you discover that you have dealt with them on
the basis of self-interest; you let them
speak when they agree with you, but you
silence them when they disagree; even

your moments of love are nothing but a barren exchange of egotisms; you talk about yourself five minutes, and he talks about himself five minutes, but if he takes longer he is a bore.

No wonder such people often say: "I must pull myself together." Thus do they confess that they are like broken mirrors, each reflecting a different image. In essence this is debauchery, or the inability to choose one among many attractions; the soul is diffused, multiple, or "legion" as Satan called himself.

3) Finally, you can use your freedom as Christ did on the Cross, by surrendering His Spirit to the Father, and as Mary bade us at Cana, by doing His Will in all things. This is perfect freedom: the displacement of self as the center of motivation and the fixation of our choices, decisions and actions on Divine Love. "Thy Will be done on earth as it is in Heaven."

We are all like limpets that can live only when they cling to a rock. Our freedom forces us to cling to something. Freedom is ours to give away; we are free to choose our servitudes. To surrender to Perfect Love is to surrender to happiness and thereby be perfectly free.

Thus to "serve Him is to reign." But we are frightened. Like St. Augustine in his early life we say: "I want to love you dear Lord, a little later on, but not now." Fearful of One Who comes to us purple-robed and cypress-crowned, we ask: "Must Thy harvest fields be dunged with rotten death?" Must gold be purified by fire? Must hands that beckon bear the red livid marks of nails? Must I give up my candle, if I have the sun? Must I give up knocking if the door of love is opened? Do we not act toward God and Mary as a child who resents the affectionate embrace of its parents, because it is not our mood to love?

Francis Thompson so reflected when he heard these words from the mouth of a child:

" 'Why do you so clasp me,
   And draw me to your knee?
Forsooth, you do but chafe me,
   I pray you let me be:
I will be loved but now and then
   When it liketh me!'
So I heard a young child,
   A thwart child, a young child
Rebellious against love's arms,
   Make its peevish cry.
To the tender God I turn:—
   'Pardon, Love most High!
For I think those arms were even
      Thine,
And that child even I.' "

As Pascal said: "There are only two
kinds of people we can call reasonable:
either those who serve God with their
whole heart because they know Him, or
those who search after Him with all their
heart because they do not know Him."

There is, therefore, some hope for those
who are dissatisfied with their choices, and
who want. If you do just that, you create

a void. Far better it is for you to say: "I am a sinner," than to say: "I have no need of religion." The empty can be filled, but the self-intoxicated have no room for God. Could we but make the surrender, we would cry out with Augustine: "Too late, O ancient Beauty, have I loved Thee," as we have discovered in the language of the great poet:

> "O gain that lurk'st ungained in all gain!
> O love we just fall short of in all love!
> O height that in all heights art still above!
> O beauty that dost leave all beauty pain!
> Thou unpossessed that mak'st possession vain."

CPSIA information can be obtained
at www.ICGtesting.com
Printed in the USA
BVHW082254291221
625115BV00002B/88